# How to Invest in Real Estate

*A practical guide with secrets and strategies to avoid mistakes and succeed in your business*

Neal Hooper

# TABLE OF CONTENTS

Flipping Properties                                          5

Hire The Right House Flipping Professionals                 13

Due Diligence Task                                          23

How To Determine Repair Estimates                           33

Common Mistakes When Estimating Repairs                     37

Common Mistakes That You Need to Avoid                      43

Managing the Rehab                                          53

Benefits of Rental Property Investing                       59

How to Analyze Rental Properties                            65

You Must Do Before Investing                                77

Make a Plan                                                 89

Location, Location, Location                               101

Conclusion                                                 109

About the Author                                           111

# Flipping Properties

The process of flipping is buying a property that is outdated and needs work. Once the work is done, you hope that the property's value has increased by more

than you spent on the improvements. Let's define a few keywords.

ARV stands for After Repair Value. It is what the flipper can sell the house for after it is fixed up.

Closing costs are what we, as a property owner, will pay when we are selling a property. Standard commissions to an agent in residential are 5%-6% of the purchase price, produced by the person selling the property. We will also have to pay legal fees, which we can estimate at 1% for this example.

Who pays what closing costs and legal fees depend on what state and county you are. Each county will have a standard split of what the buyer pays and what the seller pays, but this is all negotiable in your transaction. Some examples of closing costs include title search and transaction fees to pay the attorney or title company for their time spent helping you buy or sell the property.

These fees mean that if we sell a house for $100,000, we will only walk away with $93,000 because we had $7,000 (7%) of fees we had to pay.

Rehab budget is how much the flipper anticipates spending on the materials and labor (such as countertops, new roofs, new floors, paint, labor, and permit fees from the city if applicable). Depending on what kind of condition the house is in and how nice you want to make, the house will determine how much the rehab budget will need.

Holding costs are the expenses we are going to have to pay for owning a property. These costs include power bills, water bills, property insurance, property taxes, and other charges that come with property ownership. More in holding costs you are going to have if you own a property for long.

The final piece we need to understand is profit. It is how much the flipper would like to make from the transaction after all expenses are paid.

The flipper should buy the property according to the following formula:

ARV - Closing Costs - Rehab Budget - Holding Cost - Profit = Purchase price

If a flipper follows the above formula, they will know how much to pay for a property when a wholesaler or agent comes to them with a potential property they can buy.

**Pro Tip:** leave yourself at least a 30% profit margin as a flipper. Do not cut your profit short. If the deal doesn't work, it doesn't work. Do not bend your rules. Move on to the succeeding deal and pass up deals with thin margins. If you run into unexpected expenses you did not plan for (which you will), you do not want to be working to flip a house with no profit for yourself at the end.

Flipping a house is not investing in real estate because you are actively working on a project until it is finished. Then, to make a profit, you have to sell the product. You will only make money from a house flip when you successfully sell the property to someone else.

It is no different than what any product-based business does. It builds a product, and then to make money off it, it has to sell it. You will not have money if you do not sell the product! With house flipping, the longer you hold the house without selling it, the less money you will profit because your holding costs will rise. It is a typical business, and it is not a wrong way to do things, but we must realize that this is a different model and strategy than investing.

Please do not confuse flipping for profits by investing in building long-term wealth and monthly cash flow.

**First-time flipper mistake:** Most first-time house flippers think that they will do all the work themselves and make an extra profit because they will not pay a professional to fix the toilets or install new flooring. Often people will have to do the work themselves to make the numbers work and come out with a profit. What most people overlook in the equation is the value of their own time.

If you are an accountant that can make $50 an hour, you would be doing yourself a disservice by working on a house flip. You might think that you will reduce the expenses by doing the work yourself instead of hiring a real estate agent to do it for you. Painting is not hard; anyone can do it, including you. So why pay someone when you can do it yourself?

If your best skill is being an accountant, you should do accounting at $50 an hour because you can hire someone to paint for you at $15 an hour. By painting yourself, you are losing $50 - $15 = $35 every hour that you spend painting instead of accounting.

One of the "x-factors" that leads to a high drop out rate in house flipping is that when you have a day job and trying to flip a house is the amount of frustration you will run into. You work all day from 9-5, and then you go to work on your flip from 5- 11 pm. Your work quality is not as good as a professional, but you think doing it yourself will be cheaper.

You also really want to get the flip completed to get your payday, so you spend all day Saturday and Sunday working on completing the flip. It goes on for several months, and you quickly become exhausted and fed up with flipping. You haven't seen your friends; you haven't had a social life, haven't watched a game, haven't had quality time with your significant other.

Eventually, you get the house done, put it on the market after months of laboring, sit on the market, and wait. Your holding costs rise to where they begin to eat into your profit. You grow nervous, so you drop the price in hopes that it will sell faster.

**The flip formula for people who do it themselves looks like this:**

ARV - Closing Costs - Rehab Budget - Holding Cost - Their Time - Purchase Price = Profit

When you do any of the physical work yourself, you need to factor your time into the equation. Hence, you find out if you are making any money or having a loss instead of a profit when paid for your time on other activities.

It is the tragic story of most first-time house flippers, and I do not want you. You need to invest your money one time and get paid a profit each month for the remaining of your life without having to labor.

When you shift from house flipping for a profit to real estate investing for monthly cash flow, you will put yourself in a position to build incredible wealth, have free time, and live the dream of your life doing the things you want to do!

There is so much more to house flipping that we could talk about, but the purpose of this is to realize that house flipping can be profitable, but it is less stable and will not make you wealthy like commercial investing for cash flow will. Let's spend our time together, educating you on acquiring assets that consistently and forever put cash in your pocket.

**Pros:**

•      Profitable if done right

**Cons:**

•      Requires cash

- One-time money. Only get paid when the property sells

- Taxed as regular income if done under a year

- No tax benefits

- Not investing

- Dependent on end buyer to get paid

- Can take long periods

- Dependent on real estate values to make money

- The real estate market can change while you are in the middle of your flip

Neal Hooper

# Hire The Right House Flipping Professionals

If you plan to be in the land-flipping business for the long haul, you will have to maintain strong professional relationships with these people, so you need to shop around to find the very best ones in your area. The temptation will be to throw a dart or hire your cousin's drinking buddy, but don't. If you have to change a surveyor in the middle of a project or change any of the following horses in mid-stream, it can be incredibly disruptive and costly. Research, interview, assess.

## Title Company (aka Escrow Company or Abstract Company)

In most places, the buyer of a property will be the one to hire the legal work for the transaction. While on the other instances, it can also be a cultural matter. In some places, it's normal for the seller to provide a title insurance policy, so perhaps the two parties would decide together about it.

Sometimes the closer will be a stand-alone law firm. It will be a title company, which is generally owned by one or more attorneys and focuses solely on real estate law and, in particular, real estate transactions.

The title company is responsible for studying the title to the property, preparing the proper docs to transfer the title, and recording the signed docs with the Clerk of Court. In 'escrow,' it will also hold the money and the docs until all the dust has settled with the transaction. If you don't use a title company, you might buy a property with a mortgage on it, which the seller forgot to mention. Or you might get a faulty deed from your seller. When you buy, try always to use your regular closing company. It will be much more manageble to handle the same people. You come to trust them, and they come to trust you. So, things may be a bit more relaxed at closings.

Finding a good title company can take a while. Still, once you have a responsive and capable one, it can quickly become one of your most valuable assets as a land flipper. The reason for that is that although such a company isn't going to bend the law in your favor, it will listen and learn in your direction on minor matters of convenience, like scheduling a closing on a Friday afternoon, perhaps, or helping create the power of attorney or resolution that you need for the finish. Try to find a large, established company in your area. Have at least one short meeting with its principal(s) before making your final decision.

## *Attorney*

Decide a lawyer that specializes in real estate. He or she draws up deals and makes sure your company is in observance of local regulations. Sometimes, the title company's lawyer will also serve as your consulting attorney – for when you need a bit of simple advice, or maybe a phone call made on your behalf. But in rare cases, you may have an issue that requires a stand-alone attorney. Try to find one with connections. Or else with partners with associations. Maybe they work with the local government in some capacity or might have a seat on a vital board. You won't necessarily get any unique strings pulled, but you'll have someone who knows the system in and out. She'll know exactly who needs to be called and what argument needs to be made in your favor.

Your connection with your lawyer is one of those professional ones which can last a lifetime, so, again, when shopping around, choose carefully. Most quality lawyers will offer to talk to you for free in the first get-to-know-you meeting, especially if they think you might become a longtime client.

Keeping someone, you can contact or email for legal inquiries and consultations will be valuable as you move onwards.

### Accountant

When searching for a CPA, the most important thing is finding one who can speak English. If she can't explain to you, in pretty simple language, why she is recommending Decision A over Decision X, toss her aside and look for another. The tax code is so complex, with so much technical jargon, that you need someone who can babytalk with you.

Responsiveness is a vital characteristic to watch out for. You want a CPA who will return a phone call or email in a timely way. In your initial search, you can run a test by sending an email to every CPA on your prospect list and gauging their (non)responses. Some won't even answer. Others will consistently follow up on your inquiries.

Anyway, you have to have one. Doing business without a CPA

– at least to prepare your tax returns – is pretty much impossible. A good CPA will save you lots of money in the long run, mostly by consulting ahead of time on your projects and suggesting the best way to structure things. The accountant will help set up your business structure, track your expenses, and know what items are allowed to be written off.

### Real Estate Agent

It delivers you precise market data for the neighborhood you have chosen to flip. They have the industry understanding and provide more exact knowledge than a website for real estate. In most states, they perform on commission and are settled by the seller.

### General Contractor

Ensure that the GC is certified in the municipality you are operating in so he or she can manage your rehabs. Without a GC, you have to supervise the job zone yourself. Your timeline increases and permits room for errors, both of which sliced into earnings.

We suggest a medium-sized enterprise, one that is large adequately so that they can obtain the assignment accomplished on your timetable but small enough to recognize most of the individuals on a first-name basis.

The enterprise must be local; local to your land. It's always more useful if they know the county's laws and limitations where your land resides. They might have a satisfying working relationship with the county team members, which denotes those staffers might be slightly less moody or drag their feet during the operation.

### *Landscaper*

Employed on an as-needed basis. Almost anyone can run a bulldozer or track hoe with just a little training. Still, your landscaper is way more than a machine operator. He's a master of drainage, a builder of ponds, a solver of problems. Spotting

the difference between a mere machine operator and a guy who knows how to fix land problems – that's a skill you will acquire as you gain experience with moving dirt.

Above all, you want a landscaper who listens to you and thinks about your land problems as hard as possible. He wants to get it right and often come up with fixes that hadn't occurred to you. You want someone who is pliable but experienced. You want him to know lots more about the land than you do. You can learn from him over the years. Without a landscaper, your house may lack interest, which prevents customers, increasing your house's time on the market. It eats into your carrying expenses and decreases your ROI.

## Architect

They are only required for larger assignments, like putting additional rooms or modifying the home's layout. If an architect isn't employed, the house's foundation solidarity could become compromised, which can be valued at thousands of dollars.

## Handyman

Employed for more straightforward assignments like painting or patching spots. This person doesn't require to be certified. Employing a handyman, you don't have to pay the time and effort on a DIY task.

## Assistant

After you have satisfied with the suitable professionals and have occasional rehab assignments under your belt, you may desire to employ an assistant to assist with everyday company activities. An assistant is for the house flipper accomplishing five or more fixes and flips per year and is running a house flipping business.

## *The Utility Companies*

It pays to be in contact with the companies which control utility lines around your property. These companies should be very eager to work with you. After all, you are potentially bringing them new customers. Ask the power company about the cost and process of dropping a secondary pole onto a lot if you want temporary power while working out there. Gather as many lead as you can from the water company about the cost of a new meter, the requirements for running a supply line from their pipe on the road to a new home, etc. This information can help your lot buyers (who are usually clueless about such things) ask questions about the utilities.

Sometimes there may be utilities in the area but not adjacent to your actual property, so contacting the utility companies can become necessary. You may be astounded to learn that the water company, whose line ends three hundred feet from your property, is willing to either extend it themselves or allow you to do so. It's a chance at multiple new customers.

Sorting out the utility situation can, in some cases, add substantial value to the property, so make sure you have working relationships with the companies and people involved. At the very least, you should have all their contact info at your fingertips.

## The County

Once the survey has been done, and you have a professional drawing of your subdivision plan, you will have to go through the platting process. That means dealing with county bureaucrats. Join the local chamber of commerce, attend cocktail parties, and offer your favorite politician's support by putting up his campaign signs. We aren't talking about members of congress here. If you are employed in a rural area, the community leaders will often be highly visible. The type of people whose offices (or body shops or hair salons) you can walk into without an appointment.

Becoming known to your local area's various nabobs comes with many benefits, particularly if you can leave them with a positive impression. Not always quickly done, but it's a worthwhile endeavor that can have other consequences. You might wind up running for a local office yourself. In the end, you need the bureaucrats. So always try to make friends wherever you go. The easiest way to do that is by being friendly and upbeat yourself. It never hurts to have more acquintance, especially when you need your plat finalized by the county or your road ditches reworked.

# Due Diligence Task

Due diligence aims to verify (or perhaps not verify) all the assumptions you made during your initial evaluation of the deal. In other words, you'll be using

this time to ensure that you have all the numbers necessary to make a final go or no-go decision on this project. Much of your due diligence work should have already been completed, but perhaps not to the specificity required to make you perfectly comfortable moving forward. With that in mind, here is what should be done at this point in the purchase process:

## Get An Inspection

The inspections' goal was to generate a list of work items detailed enough to create a decent rehab estimate. You likely either did the inspection yourself, had another investor help you out, or perhaps worked with a GC to do a cursory walk- through of the property and provide some essential inspection services.

Now that you have a property under contract and consider putting a great deal of cash at risk, it's time to be a lot more formal with your inspections. The goal is to ensure that nothing significant was missed during the initial inspections that might severely impact the project schedule, budget, or scope and provide a detailed enough report to create your scope of work (SOW).

You will use this SOW to make your budget and schedule, so you need it to be complete and accurate, which all goes back to having a full inspection of the property.

At this instance, I would highly recommend spending a couple of hundred dollars on getting a full inspection completed by a well-trained property inspector. To find a good inspector, talk to other investors in your area, or even ask an excellent real estate agent. You may also want to research how property inspectors in your area are licensed and deemed qualified. For example, where I live (Georgia), there is no requirement for home inspectors to get licensed or accredited. Anyone can slap the title "Home Inspector" on themselves and start inspecting houses.

While there wasn't much in the course of national home inspector accreditation in the United States, the American Society of Home Inspectors (ASHI) is a more respected organization. If you have nothing else to go on when searching for a home inspector, at least find one that is ASHI certified, and you're probably going to do better than just picking a random inspector without any certification.

The home inspection will likely cost between $250-400, but not only is this an opportunity for you to get a full report of the problem areas of your house, but it's also an opportunity for you to start to learn the inspection process on your own. While the inspector is at the property, follow him around and ask LOTS of questions. Most inspectors will follow a similar protocol when walking through a house, and by asking lots of questions about what they are doing, what they are looking for, and what they are finding, you'll being to get a feel for the process and how to do it yourself in the future. For a few hundreds of dollars, you'll not only get an inspection report for the property, but you'll get an education to go along with it!

It is the basis for my learning to do inspections on my own. After about a half dozen home inspections and a couple of rehabs under my belt, I was comfortable inspecting pretty much every aspect of a house other than the foundation or major structural issues (I'll still call in a professional when there's a problem I'm not comfortable diagnosing myself). But, after a few houses, if you pay attention and ask a lot of questions, I promise you'll start to get much more comfortable inspecting and estimating without spending any money.

### Create A Scope Of Work (SOW)

Once you're confident that you have a firm understanding of the property's condition -- what is working and what is not working? The SOW is the detailed plan from which the entire project will be created. The SOW will determine the budget, drive the schedule, and guide the contractors. In many ways, the SOW is an essential piece of the project -- without it, the project can't come together.

### Create A Final Rehab Budget

Once your SOW is finalized, it's time to use it to create a detailed budget. Now is the time to develop a precise (and hopefully accurate) budget that will help you make a final determination about whether this project makes sense or not.

## *Verify Your Resale Value*

Now is the time to guarantee that you're confident in that value. If this is your first project or you're not very familiar with your investing area, you shouldn't hesitate to hire a professional to help you with this step.

If you can find one or two experienced real estate agents (preferably listing agents) familiar with the area to provide you a CMA, that's a significant first step. If there is any doubt that the values generated by those agents are not correct (for example, if they are far from what you estimated or if they are vastly different than one another), don't hesitate to hire a licensed appraiser to determine what the resale value of the property will be.

## *Run The Numbers Again*

With all the information you've generated above, it's now time to rerun the numbers with the new -- and hopefully more detailed information you have. The due diligence process's ultimate goal is to generate the information necessary to determine once and for all if you really should go through with the deal.

In this step, we will take the data we've generated to determine whether this property will likely generate our minimum acceptable profit should we purchase, rehab, and resell it. To determine your profit potential on this deal, we're going to rearrange The Flip Formula and plug in the numbers we generated during due diligence:

Profit = Sales Price - Purchase Price - Fixed Costs - Rehab Costs where:

Sales Price is what was determined by your final appraisal or comp analysis

Purchase Price is the contract price on the property

Fixed Costs are the final estimated costs to complete the project, minus your rehab costs

Rehab Costs are the costs to complete the rehab (your Rehab Budget)

After running the numbers using the data you've collected during your Due Diligence, you should be able to estimate the profit potential on this deal pretty accurately.

If this deal's profit potential doesn't meet your requirements, now is the time to consider other options.

## *What If The Numbers Don't Work?*

Hopefully, it won't happen too often. Still, every once in a while, you're going to find that the numbers you generate during due diligence indicate that the deal you have isn't a good deal at the agreed-upon purchase price. How you manage this situation will play a large part in whether you consistently make profits rehabbing houses or sometimes making profits.

Too many rehabbers will find themselves in a situation where they determine during due diligence that the numbers don't work but are so emotionally attached to the deal that they convince themselves it's a good deal anyway. Perhaps they'll talk themselves into believing they can sell for more than it initially thought; maybe it thinks it can cut rehab costs or believe they can get the project done more quickly to reduce holding costs. In nearly all cases, all they are doing is delaying the inevitable problems of doing a bad deal.

So, if you find yourself in an instance where you realize during due diligence that the numbers don't work, what are your options? They're pretty simple:

Ask for a price reduction. The first course of action is to go back to the seller and request a price reduction. I've found that being an honest person is the best policy in these cases – tell the seller that your initial numbers didn't work and provide some support for your realization. For example, if you realized that the resale value is lower than expected, let the seller know about recent comps that impact resale value. If your rehab costs are higher than expected, provide the seller with a list of the surprise repairs you found during due diligence. In my knowledge, if you can convince the seller that you did gather new information during due diligence that affects the deal, the seller is going to be more willing to consider a price drop than if you ask for a discount without any substantiation. For REO deals, the bank will often require inspection reports and contractor bids before considering a price reduction based on repair issues found during due diligence.

If you're unsuccessful at getting a price reduction on the deal, it's time to cut your losses and back out. It can often cause lots of hurt feelings – the seller won't be happy, your agent won't be satisfied, your contractors may not be satisfied – but temporary hurt feelings aren't nearly as bad as long-term monetary losses.

Neal Hooper

# How To Determine Repair Estimates

### *Square Footage Estimator*

It is not that hard. We have a couple of methods that are surprisingly easy to calculate an approximate repair cost. The square footage estimator is where you take the home's square footage, and you multiply it by a fixed repair cost. We always recommend $5 per square foot, at the very minimum. The house could be in perfect condition, and we are still going to assume at least $5 per square foot in repair costs. There could be hidden things that you don't know about until you buy it. If you have a property that needs a medium size rehab, you can bump that estimate up to $15-20 per square foot. If the house needs higher quality materials, we can go with $25-30 per square foot repair costs. Maybe a little more even. If it is a complete/gut rehab or needs top of the line materials, we use a $40-50 per square foot multiplier. "I couldn't believe he knew how much the repairs were. He didn't even see the house, but because he had experience in this business, he knew."

## *Each Property Is Different*

We use spreads on the sq. ft. multiplier because every house in every market in every neighborhood will be a little different. You need to understand your market and the different areas that you invest in or are buying in. Some properties are going to be rentals, and others are fix-n-flips. The value and the price of a fix-n-flip rehab home will be a lot higher than a rental. By knowing the neighborhood, we can determine what numbers we will use in the square footage estimator strategy. It is a super-easy way to assess the repairs, and it's relatively accurate. It is straightforward, don't overcomplicate it. Get out there and acquire knowledge as you go.

## Rule Of Five's

The rule of fives is a great and super-easy way to determine repairs as well. When we walk through a property, we can see that some things need work. We assign a $5000 bill to it.

It requires a roof, five-K if it needs a driveway, five-K. Suppose it needs a bathroom, five-K. Needs a kitchen, maybe five or ten-K. Don't stress yourself out by thinking it needs an $8200 kitchen and a $4300 bathroom. Five K, Ten K, Fifteen K. Boom, Boom, Boom.

It needs new windows, Five-K. If the house is big, then double it—Ten-K for a new roof, Ten-K for new siding, or Ten-K for a big driveway.

Again, know your market. The rule of fives works great for us here in the Midwest. If you live on the shorelines, you might need to bump it up to the rule of 10's.

Recap:

**Square Footage Estimator:** Determine a range for repair costs per sq. ft. based on area, type of house, and level of work that needs to be done.

Then multiply it by the sq. ft. of the home. Each Property is Different: Get to know your market. Properties can require a different level of repairs based on area, quality of materials, etc.

**Rule of Fives:** A quick and easy way to add up repair costs on the spot by using multiples of 5K

**Action Item:** Go through a house and estimate its repair costs. Use the sq. ft. method as well as the rule of fives. How do they compare? Do you like one method over the other?

# Common Mistakes When Estimating Repairs

It is essential to know what improvements are needed when building a house. There is a possibility of losing sales due to insufficient property improvement and increasing costs due to excessive improvement.

Be sure to check the refurbishments and repairs required for implementation and the following industry trends. If you have a budget that adds value to your home, incorporate the latest technology to improve heating, ventilation, air conditioning (HVAC), plumbing, electricity, appliances, and other smart homes.

### Don't Try To Be Too Big

Don't try to be too big, especially if you're not familiar with the fixed and turnaround business. Start with a detached house and rehabilitation for less than $ 50,000.

Similarly, purchasing sizeable real estate at enormous renovation investment costs is very dangerous, especially if it has just begun. It's better to start small while learning the rope.

### Don't Make Unnecessary Improvements

Modify what is needed. Improving the property too much will not give you the expected return on investment (ROI).

Keep in mind that this is a business, and you are not renovating the house to look like a dream home. However, this rule is an exception; for example, if you repair and turn a multi-million dollar house, this kind of change must be impressive.

### Choose The Right Market

No, one thing is being in the right market. If you don't choose the right market, you will kill you in the first deal. Knowing the market can help in two ways. Make the right kind of updates that the market is ready to pay.

More importantly, it is likely that buyers are waiting to purchase the final product.

So do your homework and grow the area you want to turn. Since you have to travel several times a day, it is essential to get close to home.

You also need to select the best price range for flipping.

## *Determine The Amount Of Cash Required*

Investors with little investment experience looking for hard money lenders may need to get a lot of cash in home investment. Generally, this amount ranges from 20% to 40% of sales (down payment).

However, investors can reduce this amount by negotiating a contract in which the lender acquires a portion of the profit.

If investors are experienced and have a good track record, hard money lenders are more likely to support little or no private money or a down payment from borrowers.

If the investor is new and has a small amount of money, it is necessary to get acquaintances such as family and friends to promise to collect money and profits.

Another option is to find a wealth of business partners who will pay you while you work.

## *Take Care Of All The Big Items And Work Correctly*

An infamous stigma about house fins is that they tend to cut corners. He may sin for the association, but he can give bad names to those familiar with their work. Take care of all essential items and work correctly for the first time. Potential buyers appreciate it and create an excellent reputation for your company to move forward in future deals. If you cut the corner, you can bite again.

### *Renewing Vanity*

One of the most critical improvements in repair and turning projects is the bathroom. When renewing a bathroom vanity, consider a natural colored floating vanity.

Soft and modern with rounded edges. The white quartz counter works in the bathroom. You can highlight them with a circular mirror. When selecting a cabinet color, consider shades and tones other than white. Natural nuts, mint, black, and coal are successful. Sometimes white still works. Avoid shades of gray.

### *Add Some High-End Features To The Property*

Try adding high-end functionality to low-priced properties. For example, you can add a wall-mounted hood when you update your kitchen. The extra charge is between $ 100 and $ 200, but it is much more expensive. It allows you to sell your home at the best price and get higher profits.

Data show that upgrades generally improve home sell-ability but add little or no real value.

The reason is as follows. How valuable are those beautiful new cherry wood cabinets when buyers try to tear them to replace them with white contemporary European cabinets?

There are quite exceptions to this rule of thumb. Upgrades that add areas, such as additional bedrooms and additional baths, usually add value.

Neal Hooper

# Common Mistakes That You Need to Avoid

Each retail investor dreams of beginning a real estate investment business, making money, and enjoying the "good life." Many fail to realize that investing in real

estate can be incredibly complicated and expensive if you don't know what you're doing. When you take it slowly and know how to do it properly, it can be very lucrative to invest in real estate.

## Mistake #1:

Failure to Invest in Education. Attempt to invest in infrastructure before you start paying your rent, and you need to take time to learn the fundamentals of investing in real estate. It does not mean that you need to spend thousands on training or courses related to "guru;" it means that you have to spend time researching the various investment strategies to understand what you need to do to succeed.

## Mistake #2:

Failure to set up a business. Several people begin investing with their cash, name, and credit on a small scale. What they cannot know is that any mistake could cost you all you've worked so hard to make.

Use your homework and produce a business entity that best suits your needs before you start investing. In most instances, the most appropriate company to use for your corporation will be an LLC or a Company. If something goes wrong down the road, you can cover your assets in creating a business company.

## Mistake #3:

Depending on the type of assets you own, and what you plan to do with the property, the type of coverage you will need will be decided. If you're planning to buy a single-family home for sale, you'll need to get a rental agreement. If you plan to buy and sell "Flip" property, a General Commercial Cost Plan may be the way to go as many will cover the deal's cost. For best practice, make sure that you will need you to talk to a professional insurance agent when determining which type of insurance you will need.

## Mistakes#4:

Failure to Strategize & Plan. Real Estate Investing is like any other company, so why don't you treat it like one? You need to build a clear plan of action to proceed if you want to be successful. Decide which strategy(s) works best for you before you start investing. Don't panic if it takes a while to determine the right plan, but make sure that you stick with it when you find it out.

## Mistakes#5:

Failure to find and manage a budget. One of the first things you need to do is find out how much cash you need to spend. If you only have enough money for a condo, don't try to buy an apartment complex. Once you've worked out how much money you've got to spend, concentrate your time and energy on a budget that fits your needs. If you're over-budgeting, your growth potential may be reduced. If you're under budget, you're most likely going to get into trouble, resulting in a large amount of debt.

## Mistake #6:

Failure to Correctly Estimate the Cost of Repairs. Not only will this mistake cost you time, but it can also cost you the whole deal. Invest in a local contractor to inspect the property to provide you with a list of improvements that will be required and the cost of completing every repair if you are looking to purchase a house. It will save you time on the back end and thousands of dollars.

## Mistake #7:

Failure to create a team. Everyone heard the saying, "You're just as good as the weakest link." If you're trying to invest in real estate and don't have a strong team behind you, you will be the weakest link. It is essential to surround yourself with a great group of people and to continue to have an excellent working relationship with these people. Developing your team can take a lot of time and energy, but demonstrate your progress when you're finished.

## Mistake #8:

Failure to take action. After educating yourself, starting a business, securing insurance, defining a strategy or project, developing a budget, and establishing your team, nothing is left to put everything to work and take action. At first, it might be daunting. You might make little mistakes, but if you don't take action, you're never going to make money and be successful. It can be challenging to invest in real estate, and if you go wrong, it can be costly. Investing in real estate, on the other hand, can be very professional and financially beneficial. Don't be afraid to ask a specialist for assistance. If you know what you're doing, most of these errors can be prevented. The more information you acquire and research, the fewer errors you make.

## *How to Automate Your Rental Investing Business*

One thing you'll see when you invest in Real Estate is that there's a lot of work to do to get a deal done, and the weather you're a rehabber or a wholesaler, and you've got to do a lot of work before it's sold. You usually have more time than cash at the start of most shareholder companies, and you end up doing everything yourself to keep down your costs and increase your profits. Heck, marketing itself is costly enough, and if you have little or no money to start with, you're forced to do all you can to get your first contract.

That's fine, and nearly everyone starts that way, but you don't always want to stay that way, even if by doing so, you can make a more significant piece of the pie. But why is this? If I could save money and make more per deal, why wouldn't I want to do it all myself?

There's a straightforward reason why you want to pay someone else to do certain things and why working on others is essential to you.

The simple answer is not the same as all the tasks of an investment real estate business. Saying the same word in another way, some jobs are simple enough that anyone can do them while others need the ability to think, invent, lead, and communicate.

And back to my original question as to why you don't want to do this independently.

Focusing on essential tasks and contracting out the bottom and eventually, middle-level tasks for others is simply more productive. It is attributable to something called "hourly pay." When you spread your time doing all aspects of the business, you take your hourly wage and average it from the whole pie.

If, on the other hand, you only perform the essential tasks and contract the rest at a low price, you will produce more, and your hourly wage will rise. It is the main difference between a sole owner and a businessman and why the businessman ends up making money.

I don't know about you, but I got to make money and have a ton of free time in this business!

Let me give you an excellent example of what I'm thinking about. My husband and I primarily sell the MLS and Craigslist in two different locations to find all of our offers. Both of these places are necessarily free to market (yes, I know the MLS costs money every year, but let's say it's free from there... deal? after the fee is paid). And, every day, we can spend hours sending lowball deals to the MLS and advertising on Craigslist to get people to call in.

Then every day, we can spend hours dealing with Realtors ' answers and sellers ' calls. All you need to find a deal, and that's when it all happens at once! Now you're having to do daily tasks like putting up advertisements and making offers on the MLS, coping with emails and calls in addition to putting together the deal so that you can either sell or rehabilitate it. What's most likely to happen is that the lower tier activities cease while you're focused on the tasks that make you money, and when you make that money, you've got to start all over again.

Here is what I suggest, hire a Virtual Assistant after you make your first or even second deal, and you've got some money to play with now! When we did that, our production skyrocketed, and there was a decrease in the amount of work we had to do, and all that work was the tedious work we hated doing!

Now we have a lady over in India who works for $2.25 an hour with a Masters's degree making offers on the MLS. Have you heard me there? She's got a Master Dang, and she's working for

$2.25 an hour!

Try to see if you can get a homeless man to work for the cheap one. Ha! Even if you could bet a month's wages, he wouldn't put in the same effort and enthusiasm as the lady with her degree we have in India;) She's extraordinarily productive and very smart and can send 50-60 offers to the MLS within 2 hours.

We started working 10 hours a week with her, and she was worth her gold weight! Think about it, and we've got about 250-300 deals for about $25 each week. We made her do more research as time went by, while we focused on the creative tasks (which are also more enjoyable and take less time) high!

Necessarily, Virtual Assistants are people who can perform any function you request of them that can be done on an internet-connected device.

Someone who sends an offer to the MLS or places an ad on Craigslist does NOT have to be in my office, nor do I have to see them know they are doing their job. We let her use our company email to send deals, and we can track her progress by merely checking the sent folder to see what she's doing so limited oversight. So, anywhere in the world, this person can be! How many of us wanted to work with our jobs from home, but it never seemed that the bosses were on board for it?

We can now be the "hot" boss and, as a result, reap the rewards! You can do all the menial tasks once you have someone on board and let you concentrate on the things that will make you money, like bringing together buyers and sellers! The larger you get, the more tasks you need your Virtual Assistant to delegate. You can eventually get an "apprentice" real estate investor who can do everything you need, including managing your Virtual Assistant. A wage plus a percentage of profits can be paid to him.

# Managing the Rehab

*Take Pictures, Measure Everything, And Decide What Needs To Be Done*

When done without a system, rehabbing requires a great deal of time to master and execute. What's even worse is that most investors start with limited experience, let alone a system to follow.

The average investor enters into rehabbing, having done work on their home.

Learning how to renovate properties and manage contractors requires you to commit and adhere to a proven track record system. If you are eager to commit the time to master and train, you will get the opportunity to cash in on some of the most significant checks in the real estate business.

Your first project should be a cosmetic renovation. Focus your attention on less intimidating tasks such as paint, carpet, and other purely aesthetic elements. As your project experience grows, you can take on larger, more involved projects. Start small and build your expertise gradually to keep from the getting in over your head.

The more rehabs you do, the more experience you will achieve—and the less costly mistakes you'll make. Most importantly, it will drastically increase your chances of achieving early success in your investing endeavors.

The most critical actions in growing your rehab business are learning, understanding, and mastering the entire rehab process and system—which means that you won't be spending all of your time on the job site. Throughout the process, you will also start to develop relationships with contractors and subcontractors. Good contractors are the most critical team members for building and growing your residential redevelopment business.

Contractors are as much as our customers as their customers when it comes to renovating properties—don't forget that.

Preparation is the key to stay on schedule and within budget for a rehab. You have to develop a good plan of what renovations and improvements you want to undertake before involving a contractor. You must also have a clear picture of your budget to establish a realistic scope of work.

### *Prepare for Your Rehab*

It will be your initial visit to the property once you own the deal. In one stop, the goal is to gather all the information and necessary details to put together the work scope used to bid and hire contractors to do the job. On this visit, you must accomplish these three tasks:

Take pictures of everything and anything you think will need improvement.

Make necessary measurements to any rooms that you may change the layout.

Start making final decisions on precisely what you need to do on the rehab to sell your subject property.

One of your most crucial tasks to complete during this first walkthrough after you close on the property is to identify the items you need to fix and help sell the house when complete. For example, should you remove a non-loadbearing wall between the kitchen and living room or add a window to take advantage of a good view? Should you add a skylight to add brightness to a dark room? These are just a sample of the decisions that now need to be finalized before you start the rehab with your identified contractor team—not in the middle or after. The succeeding list of the items to take with you to prepare an accurate work scope.

**Camera.** Capture areas with problems so you can refer to them as you prepare your scope of work. It will also give you "before" pictures to illustrate the improvements that you have made. It's rewarding to see the by-products of your work, so preserve photo records of each assignment.

**Flashlight.** Whether the power is turned on at the property, or you ought to examine dark crannies and nooks, a flashlight is still essential. You don't want to squander a trip and not be able to finish the walkthrough.

**Graph Paper and Tape Measure.** You'll need to make a to- scale illustration of the house, particularly of the spots you plan to repair. It allows you to generate portions for your scope of work.

**Lockbox with Spare Key.** It will prevent you from meeting your contractor to grant access at the property and authorize you to dispatch contractors to the property to organize their bids.

**Marketing Materials.** You can generate a motivated buyer leads with "We Buy Houses" or "For Sale" signs to build your buyers' list. However, even if you set up a "For Sale" sign, don't let possible customers view the property until renovations are done.

## *Property Walkthrough*

Break your walkthrough down into the same units you will use for your work scope based on the property repair estimate sheet: exterior, interior, and mechanicals. It will keep the walkthrough systematic and prevent you from overlooking spaces that require attention.

Begin by approaching the home's exterior as a potential buyer would. Notice everything that gives you a negative impression. Low landscaping, decrepit fencing, and peeling paint are just some of the items that can put off interested customers before they ever step in the door. Also, consider objects such as new sod or an outdoor seating area that can be counted to improve the property's value. Ensure all external lights function and examine irrigation systems and mechanical garage door openers if they are existing.

Begin the process again on the house's interior. Pay attention to the first thing you notice and feel when you walk in the home. How can you improve the wrong impression or enhance a good impression? Go through each room and take note of every detail imaginable to get an accurate idea of exactly how much effort needs to be done a second time with the property repair estimate sheet, but with much greater detail. You will need this data when preparing your scope of work.

Measure and sketch areas of the property where you may want to change the layout, such as the bathrooms or kitchens, and include any specific problem areas. Note the location of mechanical system items such as the water heater and the furnace.

# Benefits of Rental Property Investing

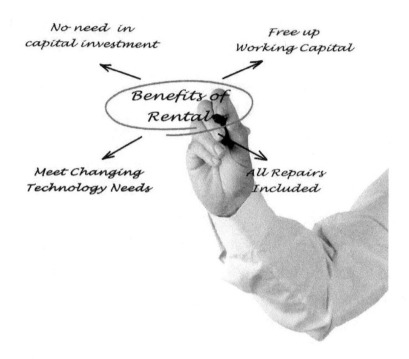

Investment properties offer many great benefits. Some are subtle, like the idea of creating financial security. Others are very concrete in dollars and cents. But most are specific that put dollars in your bank account.

The most noticeable benefit is that someone else pays your mortgage and builds up capital for you. If you buy a property with positive cash flow and use a good strategy to ensure that your vacancies are very low, the property's income covers your mortgage costs. Over time, you build equity with little effort on your part because the loan pays for the principle.

That is the easiest way to build wealth globally, and why rental property ownership is the most crucial strategy for most of the world's wealthiest investors.

Another advantage is to deduct the rental fee. Owning real estate investments as a business venture allows you to deal with many items, such as company expenses. Change some of your costs for Your mobile phone, internet service, car, and even your house is possible with a real estate company. Depreciation "costs" usually allows you to display a "depreciation" when your property increases in value. When you sell, capital gains tax is often lower than comparable wages. Generally, the tax benefits of owning real estate allow you to live a better lifestyle while showing a lower income.

A third advantage of investing in real estate in real estate is that it is not very fluid. Now some people see this as a mistake. However, this can be seen from a different perspective. When stock prices fall rapidly, investors often refrain from selling assets.

That is easy to do, and the exchanges will sell at the lowest prices instead of having a long-term strategy. If you have a home that provides positive cash flow, you are usually not tempted to sell if some prices fall. You normally wait.

Unless you go through a divorce, you can usually sell your property on your terms.

On the other hand, this lack of liquidity often puts desperate people in a bad situation. If a seller has a personal circumstance that forces them to sell, they are often willing to sell properties below market value. It allows you to earn a significant profit on the date of purchase. Many real estate investors say, "you make your money when you buy," which is true. Buy only properties from motivated sellers, and you will surely build your net worth.

## *Smart Rental Property Investments*

Investing in rental housing is an entirely different story today compared to just a few years ago. The current challenging state of the economy makes it more important to have real estate investment knowledge than ever before to make your investments successful.

Know your neighborhood: What is the demographic data of the area where your future home is located. It includes the average age and income of residents, levels of education, etc. It gives you information about the available rental housing in the area. The relationship with the neighborhood and whether it improves or falls also needs to be known. If you notice that it falls into disrepair, don't run away from the property! It's not worth risking your hard-earned money, no matter how promising investment is, the seller might tell you.

Prepare your "homework" in advance: Before you start buying rental properties, you must first get to know the business's basic rules.

It includes learning from tenants and tenants, understanding your rights and responsibilities as a homeowner, knowing the tenants' rights and responsibilities, and developing necessary repair and maintenance capabilities. Hire a Qualified Property Lawyer: If a property lawyer represents you during the sales transaction, you can prevent many potential problems for you. It is easier to hire a lawyer to "keep you out of trouble" than hiring someone to "help you out of trouble."

Hiring an expert attorney (and one you feel comfortable with) can be an excellent "insurance policy" to protect the most significant financial transaction you are likely ever to make.

Proof of Real Estate: Do not rely on the seller's oral statements (or the seller's agent) on the cost of ownership. Play safely instead: Receive copies of "actual invoices" and invoices to verify the cost of using the property. Vendors can sometimes underestimate expenses and exaggerate rental income to justify a higher selling price for their property erroneously. Tenant Information: As a buyer, you have the right to obtain rental information about the tenants of the property.

It includes rental agreements or rentals and any deposits and prepaid rent paid to the current owner. That information can be obtained by sending "estoppel letters" to the tenants. Renting a Reputable Property Inspector: A good inspector determines the property's overall condition and reveals any faults or problems that need to be repaired or replaced.

The cost of repair or replacement work that may be necessary can be high. It must generally be deducted from the sales price or negotiated with the seller. Develop a "long-term" investment view: Patience is a virtue, and if you develop this property, you will earn good rewards in the future - the pot o- gold at the end of the rainbow is waiting for you! The race wins slowly and steadily. Resist the temptation to join "get rich quick crowd," and you don't have to worry about being left out in the cold!

In short, the road to success in investing real estate in real estate can present many phrases along the way. It can certainly be made much smoother and less risky by including the above investment recommendations

Neal Hooper

# How to Analyze Rental Properties

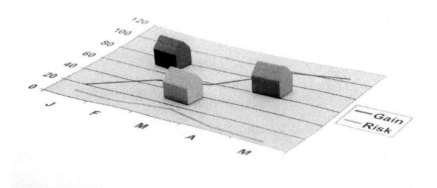

Cash flow and appreciation are the two things you should look at when analyzing properties. Cash flow is the money left over after the bills have been paid. Your

cash flow is what will determine if the property is right for you. It is what you calculate to see what capital is left at the end of the month after everything has been paid out.

### *Speculation*

To the real estate market, speculating means assuming the property will increase in value and that you can cover the costs, which can be stressful, given the volatility of the market. There is little need for this guesswork. More technology has become available in apps that can calculate mortgage costs, expenses, and help you plan to cover them in their entirety. The biggest reason for beginners being unsuccessful in this venture is underestimating their costs. The renter covers some, but what's left are capital expenditures and will be paid by you over the life of ownership.

## What is Income?

It is the fair market value of what you can charge for rent. It is based on location, type of property, how many bedrooms and bathrooms, what kinds of amenities there are, its size, etc.

All of this will help determine what you charge for the property or unit. It isn't to say you add everything up that you will be out of pocket for and charge that amount to recoup your costs. It means checking out what the market will bear for a current rental price. You don't want to undervalue the unit or property, as you run the risk of finding tenants that don't value it the same as you, and overvaluing the property runs the risk of it remaining vacant.

## What Is an Expense?

Expenses are the 'out-of-pocket-expenses' that go into owning and running a property. For instance, let's say you bought a property, and your mortgage was $800/month. You decide that the market will bear you charging $1000/month, so you believe that you have a cash flow of $200/month.

It can get tricky when accounting for the vacant rates, capital expenditures, repairs, and a property management company (if you use one). Try to average them out, so when something happens, you're not thrown off. Maintaining good records will help track and calculate your various expenses to average your costs better over the years. Whether you are you doing this yourself or have an accountant managing it for you, the better records you keep, the easier it will be during tax time.

## Vacancy Rates

While it's impossible to estimate how many units might be vacant at any given time, you will need to understand that it will happen at some point. Now, how long they stay empty will depend on your area and how good you are at advertising your available units. If you think it could be for longer than a month or two months, you need to add the expense into your calculation, so you're not out of pocket for those months the unit is empty. You can talk to any local property management company for starters if you don't have one and find out what they average for vacancy rates. Once you know the typical vacancy rate, you can start to break it down as a percentage.

Let's say you charge $1000/month for rent. You have found out that the vacancy rate is approximately 5%. You will divide $1000 by 5% or 0.05 to get $50. It is what you will want to set aside in your vacancy rate contingency fund.

## Repairs

Repairs can be tough to estimate. A single-family home built in 1944 will need more repairs than a home under 20 years ago. A recently rehabbed building will require less regular maintenance than an apartment building neglected by owners for many years. Similarly, we can never estimate how much we will need an unexpected vehicle repair other than routine maintenance required once a year; the same can be said for a rental property. A general rule of thumb for vehicle repairs is approximately $150/month, so translating that to property repairs is 5% - 15% depending on the building's age. Keep in mind this is an average; every building is different.

## Capital Expenditures

These are the "big" ticket items that you can't always plan for but know you will need to deal with at some point over the life of your ownership. They don't need to be replaced often, but they typically cost a fair amount when they do. Things such as roof repair or replacement, appliances, plumbing, electrical systems, windows, driveways, etc.

These can be hard to budget for because a lot of it will depend on the age of the building or house you purchase and the age of expenditures at the time of purchase.

## A "Good" Rental Property

This is a highly subjective topic. Each investor will have their ideas of what makes a property "good" outside of the potential to earn decent cash flow. There is no "perfect" property, just one that helps you achieve your financial goals. So, given all the information above about expenses and income, what does it take to have a suitable property?

## Attribute

Attributes are the things that prospective tenants are looking for in a home, and you want to consider bringing in the steady, stable, long term tenants you are looking for.

### Enough bedrooms

I recommend at least three per house. Two is standard depending on the area, but if your tenants are a young couple looking to build a family, they will soon run out of space, and you will be looking for new tenants before you know it. Any more, and you will need to target a specific market of a tenant with either a large family or is wealthy.

### The age of the house

Older homes are less expensive upfront, but the cost comes sooner with pricey repairs. Because of this, you want to be aware that tenants may not be happy about higher heating bills, making it harder to rent out. Newer homes, of course, have a higher purchase price but require less maintenance with fewer issues needing repair in the long term.

### Utility price

It's an excellent strategy to require the tenant to pay these. Personal habits or "creature comforts" vary, so there is always the chance of the electric bill skyrocketing in the summer by leaving all of the windows open with the A/C running 24 hours a day. While tenants will be careful and honest about the bills, you don't want to risk it, make sure they know what you cover, and anything else is their responsibility.

## An outdoor area

If you can find something with a small outdoor space such as a patio or side yard, then you've hit the jackpot. Recreational space is essential, so if your prospective property doesn't have one, I recommend making sure it's at least close to a park and mention it in your property rundown.

## Parking

Always a plus to have space for your tenants to park at least one car, whether it's a driveway, carport, or garage. It's better than street parking with growing traffic congestion, especially in the city, tenants might not be willing to risk damage to their vehicles.

## *Problems to Consider*

First, try not to see them as problems, but challenges instead. It's all about morphing how you look at what you own and what they can do for you in cash flow. Most of the "problems" listed below others may walk away from as they are considered too difficult or not worth the trouble. This method can make it more manageable for you to get a better deal on the property. Don't forget to include these repairs in your budget as they will increase the property's value. Pricing out new or unfamiliar repairs may seem like a daunting task, so here is some clarity on those challenging projects.

- **Old house stench**

That smell tells you that this house is old, musty, or something died here as soon as you open the door.

- **Old carpets**

You can try steam cleaning it yourself, but it's easier to have the carpets and underlay replaced as you are required to do as a landlord.

- **Stained tile**

Clean all the laminate or tile floors thoroughly in the kitchen and bathroom(s) with a heavy bleach and water solution.

- **Cleaning**

Do an overall cleaning from top to bottom of the entire house. I would recommend hiring a cleaner to do the job for you. If you decide to do it yourself, start with washing the walls, even if they don't look dirty at first glance.

- **Painting**

After the walls are clean, patch up any holes or dings and make sure to use a primer, such as Kilz Primer, to eliminate any lingering odors. Apply a fresh coat of paint, and your room will look brand new.

- **Out of date kitchen**

While replacing appliances isn't cheap, but they are an easy fix. Painting old dark cupboards and replacing the hardware is less than a day's work, low cost, and will dramatically improve your interior's look. New counter-tops can be purchased prefab from stores like Home Depot and Lowe's for just a few hundred dollars

- **Bad roof**

While having a leaky, cracked, or old roof may sound daunting and can get expensive, you can shop around for deals.

- **Mould**

Mould can be a death sentence for infrastructure if you let it go for too long. Mould appears when there is an excess of moisture, so if you can pinpoint, fix, and clean up the moisture problem, it's not so scary.

- **Overgrown Yards**

If the yard looks like a tangled jungle of a mess, it won't be appealing to prospective tenants who may worry they have to clean it up.

### *Financial Consideration*

Once you have chosen your property, it's time to examine the financial considerations, such as income, expenses, and debt. It requires a fair amount of paperwork and calculations, but a bit of time upfront will help make the decision easier and run less risk of making the wrong decision about the property.

• Gross scheduled income

• Vacancy & credit loss

• Gross operating income

• Operating expenses

Subtract expenses from the gross operating income gives you the net operating income. It is the income before financing or income taxes and after vacancy and expenses.

Another factor to consider is the Capitalization Rate (Cap Rate), which is the most common way to assess profitability and return potential. It represents what a property will yield over a one-year time frame. However, this is assumed on an unleveraged property, one that is purchased upfront with all cash. The most straightforward formula is:

**Cap Rate** = Net Operating Income/Current Market Value

• Net Operating (expected) Annual Income, minus all expenses

• Market Value (present-day value of the asset as per market rates)

Various things can affect the cap rate and change it significantly over the years. Real estate is risky, but the return can be worth it.

Now, as with anything in real estate, there are going to be risk factors. These could include

- Age, location, and status of the property

- Regular rentals versus vacancy

- Property type

- The overall market rate of the property

One way to keep the cap rate high is to buy in low-income areas. It may put the property in a lower class than I suggested buying in before, but it is one way to start your portfolio for less than expected and get the cap rate high for resale. Properties that you can purchase for cheap and revamp will appreciate it. Low cap rates mean less risk and buying newer properties that don't require any work could see a lower return.

# You Must Do Before Investing

## Evaluate Your Finances

The step you need to take before investing in a rental property is to evaluate your finances. There is nothing that can be purchased without your finances being in

place. Regardless of whether you only have enough of a deposit for one property and an additional amount for any repairs and renovations, if they're needed, you need to analyze how an investment into a rental property will relate to your finances.

To set yourself up as an investor, you need to prepare a personal income statement that outlines your finances. It means that you list the income you presently have

After all, the income is accounted for and add in any savings you have to that number. Then subtract all the essentials you pay for – mortgage/rent, electric, water, heat, etc., and all other debts you have. The net number will give you a prominent picture of the finances you have that can be used to invest in a real estate property that will become your rental and money set aside for repairs and maintenance.

Your financial statement will give you a total picture of your finances. You know what your responsibilities are, and now you have your real estate business finances in place. It will be your investment capital. Once you know how much investment capital you have, the question is, how much of it should you invest, and how much of it will be put aside for repairs? The answer is within the capital you have, the decision you'll make about what amount of a budget you will feel comfortable carrying and doing the math.

It's essential to understand that even if the investment is for only one rental property, you know exactly your parameters when you invest. What you don't want are any financial difficulties from the very first time out of the gate.

## *The Investment Plan*

This plan will be a guideline based on investing in a single-family home that will be a rental property. It will take you through the financial steps you need to follow in preparation to invest in a property.

If you've decided on how much investment capital will be used to purchase a property, you need to develop an outline of steps to take and assign the amount of money that is included in the plan:

Remember that the competition for investment properties is fierce, so having your funding in place allows you the opportunity to make an immediate offer on a property.

All other costs connected to the investment, including repairs, will be determined once you have found a property and the value of the property is in place:

- Property and liability insurance

- Property taxes

- Inspection and appraisal costs

- Closing costs, attorney, and accountant fees

- Property management service fees

The cost of permits that may be needed to do renovations before the property is ready to rent.

Permits are necessary for renovations such as a roof, upgrading a kitchen, or a bathroom. Permits are not required to paint the interior of the property.

Check with the local municipality what permits are necessary and the pricing for permits before you have any work done. Use licensed contractors who specialize in the work you will be having done. They should also know what permits are necessary. You or the contractor will file the permit, and you will pay for it.

- Repair costs incurred during pre-rental repair work

- Post-rental funds for any future repairs

If your proposal for a property is accepted, then all the other costs – the property and liability insurances, property taxes all additional fees listed will be more defined and give you a more concrete idea of the property investment's total cost.

## Cost Property inspection

A lender will make it mandatory that an inspection is performed before the closing. The cost maybe more for a much larger home and reduced to as little as $200 to inspect condominiums and small homes under 1,000 square feet. Homes that are approximately 2,000 square feet will cost roughly $400 or more.

Depending on the region of the country you are located in the U.S., additional inspections, such as for mold, termites, radon, termites, and the like, may impact the inspection.

The inspection can determine the problem. Suppose the inspector gives you a determination of what it will take to remedy the problem and an estimate of what the cost would be to do so. In that case, you can move forward with the transaction as long as you are staying within your investment budget and feel the repair does not cost restrictive.

However, suppose the inspection shows that a problem is too overwhelming to be fixed within a reasonable amount of time and within what you have as investment capital. In that case, you can pull out of the contract with no penalty and have your deposit returned to you in full.

### Property and liability insurance

The insurance cost is based on the home's size, the price of the property you will be paying, and where the property is located.

Based on nationwide annual average cost for home insurance can be $1,228 for a property valued at $200,000 with a deductible of $1,000 and $100,000 liability coverage and $1,244 for a $200,00 valued property with $1,000 and

$300,000 liability coverage. When researching the insurance costs, you need to adjust this information to the county and city where the property was purchased and speak with a reputable insurance agent to get the best coverage rates.

### Closing costs

The cost to close on a property can range anywhere from 2%- 5% of the property's purchased price.

### Legal and Financial Coverage

Find a good real estate lawyer whose practice focuses on real estate investing and law. Consult with a lawyer who will work with you on a project-by-project basis; it's always wise to have a lawyer to advise you on real estate law.

Hire a licensed accountant to keep track of your real estate capital and can give you a financial picture of your property and how profitable (or not) it is.

### Purchasing the Property with Cash

Cash is king in purchasing real estate. Using money eliminates all the procedures and formalities that banks and mortgage brokers. If you are buying a property with cash, you need to show proof of funds, submitting bank statements, and any other information from financial institutions where you have funds.

You need to submit copies of statements from each of these accounts to verify you have the cash to purchase the property. Additionally, the funds must be more than the offer you're making for the property.

Purchasing a real estate investment property with cash can be processed and closed rather quickly. Sellers usually analyze offers from investors who will pay some money for their property over those financed offers.

### *Financing the Investment Property Transaction*

For investment purposes, loans are conventional loans and defined by having your property investment purchase funded by a full-service bank, mortgage broker, or credit union. 20% of the purchase price is required as a down payment.

There are several reasons that the amount of the down payment is considerably high yet is required. It is to cover the rise lending institutions take when they lend on investment properties. It is also to protect your assets. Some other reasons are:

## Private mortgage insurance

Banks require a 20% deposit of the price of an investment property being purchased. If the deposit is lower than the required amount, there will be additional private mortgage insurance tax charges

## Interest Rates

The higher the deposit, the lower the interest rate. Additionally, if you want to lower the interest rate, you can even do what is known as "buy down" the interest rate by buying an exciting point.

For example, your loan interest rate is 5.75%, the interest rate for an investment property mortgage. You want to pay a lower interest rate over the life of the loan. You decide to "buy a point." The one point is valued at 1% of the mortgage, which is valued at $1,000 for every $100,000.

This buy down can be paid before the loan is finalized. When you buy one point, your mortgage's interest rate will be 4.75% over the loan's life. It makes quite a difference in your monthly mortgage paid each month.

You may wonder why interest rates on an investment property are higher than on properties that are purchased as a primary residence. In actuality, mortgage borrowers tend to bail out from the rental property before they would ever bail from their primary residence if the investment property doesn't work out.

Lenders are mindful that a borrower who invested in a property used for a business purpose is less attached. Investors are 30% more likely to bail on a mortgage than owners who occupy the property.

## Learn to Have Patience

A real estate investor making their first investment loan with a lender will need to have patience while the loan is studied and eventually finalized. Banks don't make their funding transaction decisions very quickly.

The investor's finances, credit score, and cash reserve are all scrutinized by the bank and are revised more than once before the loan is finally forwarded to the underwriter to be approved. There is still the possibility that the loan will be rejected even after it has been looked over again and again because the underwriter because, in the bank's opinion, it is too uncertain and risky to be funded.

## *Mortgage Company Funding*

Mortgage companies are known as the middleman to numerous lenders. The investor is matched to a lender who fits their needs by a mortgage broker. If the loan is accepted, the mortgage broker steps back from the transaction, and the lender, who is the originator of the loan, will work directly with the investor.

Mortgage brokers are subject to the lenders' regulations that they deal with and do not control any limitations or restrictions a lender may have. Additionally, when you use a mortgage broker, some fees are paid to both the broker and the lender. These fees may be high with the loan originator.

Depending on the country you reside in, the loan amount is how the fees are established. Remember that brokers have a varied range of lenders to work with but may focus on those who offer the best commission paid to them. The lender pays the contract to the agent for bringing the loan to them

## *Short Term Loans*

This loan is known as a "hard money" short term loan and is secured by the real estate that you are purchasing or, with more seasoned investors, a number of their real estate investments already in place.

The loans will be provided by a group of investors or a single private investor independent of banks, mortgage brokers, or credit unions.

You secure the loan with real estate. The lenders viewed the loans as an investment, and the real estate is the transaction's insurance. There is no concern about the investor defaulting on the loan. If they do, the lender seizes the property and sells it.

This information is what you need to prepare for the first steps you will take as a first-time investor. It outlines all the essentials you need to know about financing, finding the right funding, understanding the loans and their terms, all the benefits and the disadvantages of the risks in rental property investing, and learning how to make practical decisions about real estate investment.

# Make a Plan

It can be tempting to get an idea and then jump right into a real estate purchase. With your mind focused on the bottom line, it is easy to forget the practical steps. You want to get in and get started as fast as you can. While you may luck out and find a good deal, it is also a pretty easy way to put yourself on the fast track to disaster. The best method to evade this kind of failure is to build your real estate business plan.

Unlike the regular property owner, you won't just buy one piece of property, and you're done. If you're interested in developing a real estate empire, you will be jumping from one great opportunity. You'll probably be pretty successful for the first one or two properties, but things can get quite complicated after that. As you create your plan, there are a few things you need to include.

## *Your Purpose for Investing*

•      A dream vacations

•      Improve your quality of life

•      Build a retirement fund

•      Your child's university education

It can be complicated to stay focused without a sense of direction. You will end up looking at investments that won't help you achieve your plans.

After you've determined your purpose, your next step should be to decide what type of investments you're going to be focused on.

•      Student rentals

•      Multi-family rentals

•      Rent to own properties

•      Vacation rentals

•      Flipping houses

The key reason for developing a plan is to treat your real estate investments as an entire business. If you're planning on using this for income, it will be a whole business, and you should start with this approach in mind from the very beginning.

Regardless of the kind of business it represents, every business plan must have clear intentions on what the investor hopes to do, what they hope to get out of it, and why they want to do it. Writing out your plan is not just to help you remember these things, but it is also a way to keep your eyes trained on your end goal.

But this does not mean that you have to write out a complex and detailed plan complete with financial statements, tax records, or other complicated documents to get started. You first list your significant milestones and then break each milestone down into smaller and smaller manageable steps.

Here is an example of a basic outline that you can follow:

1.     **Mission Statement**

- What is your business?

- What kind of benefits will you provide?

- What is the purpose of your business?

- I want to          for

2.     **Vision**

- Where do you perceive yourself in the future?

- What is your dream?

- Mental Picture

- My business will    by    in 5 years

- Create a vision board

3. **Goals**

- What do you anticipate to achieve with your real estate investing?

- It may seem like the same thing as step 2, but here you want to go into more detail. Be very specific

- Examples:

    o To get a more pleasant home

    o A dream vacation to Fiji

    o Retirement fund

    o Go back to school

    o Travel the world

4. **Time Frame**

- Set a detailed timeline for each goal

- Prioritize

5. **Type of Property**

- Student Rentals

- Multi-family

- Rent to Own

- Starter Homes

- Buy and Hold

- Tiny Homes

- Container Homes

- Collapsible Homes

- Flips

- Choose one to focus on

- Master the strategy before starting another

6.  **Rules**

- Rules to look for deals

- Distance from home – Only consider properties within 20 minutes from home

- No HOA fees

- Cash flow minimum

- No underground tans

- # of bedrooms

- 1+ bathrooms

7. **Market**

- Location – Neighborhood

- Know the area

- Travel time

- Travel expenses

8. **Team**

- Who is on your team?

- Business Partners

- Support system

- Banker

- Lawyer

- Insurance broker

- Home inspector

- Realtor

- Property manager

9. **Financials**

- Investment capital

- Where is the money coming from?

- Live in a while fixing

- Home Equity

- Cash

- Securities

- Business Partners

10. **Exit Strategy**

- How will you collect money?

- Pay off mortgage

- Rent

- Flip

- Rehab

- Rent to own

- Always have more than one strategy

When you break up your business plan into segments like the example above, it won't feel so overwhelming, and you can take it in small bite-sized pieces that are easily manageable. As you gain more experience in real estate, you will find that your plans will become more detailed but more manageable at the same time.

## *Rental Property*

The rental property uses the property to obtain a regular income from those who choose to rent or lease. It is a magnificent method to make a stable revenue. Unlike the flipping method, where you fix and sell, you will receive a smaller income over a long term.

There are numerous ways in which you can create a steady income through rentals. If you purchase and manage the property, you can rent it out for the long term. Its method will give you a steady flow of revenue that could last you the long term.

Another way you can make money on rental properties is to offer the home on a rent-to-own plan. Its system is where the renter gives you a down payment and pays you to rent with the specific agreement that a percentage of the rent will be applied to the home's sale price. At an agreed-upon time, the renter can either return the property to you or pay it off based on the contract terms.

You are not restricted to renting out apartments and homes. You can also rent out condos, townhouses, commercial property, and even land. With either option, you will receive a monthly income applied to the mortgage, interest, and maintenance needed to keep the property in livable condition.

## *Flipping*

With all the T.V. shows now, many people are very excited about flipping houses. Finding a distressed property at a discount and then improving it and reselling seems like a real easy way to make some fast money. When you fix and flip, you find a structurally sound home but needs some cosmetic work to bring up its resale value. It could be as simple as a nice coat of paint to refinish the floors, upgrading the kitchen or lighting fixtures.

Flipping properties is an excellent way for beginners to enter the real estate game. It comes with shallow risk because you can usually find homes that have been abandoned and get them at ridiculously low prices. After putting in a little extra cash, you can turn quite a sizable profit in just a matter of a few months.

Older homes and foreclosures are usually the most popular choices, but you don't have to limit yourself to these areas. These work great, primarily if you have skills in carpentry, electrical, plumbing, etc.

## *Set Up Bank Accounts*

For your money to flow freely in real estate, you need to have a healthy relationship with your banking partners. A robust and lasting relationship is more important in this industry than in any other.

You will soon discover that you will rely on your bank for many aspects of your business. Aside from paying contractors, realtors, and other services, you will depend on you will need several different banking accounts to keep your business afloat. Thus, you have to be very mindful in selecting a bank that will manage your business accounts. It would be smart to learn how to negotiate for the best interest rates you can find.

## *Interest Rates*

Good credit terms will be crucial to the success of your business. Interest rate spreads and other alternative financing plans can vary wildly from one institution to another, especially when dealing with the company. It is crucial to lessen the risk of exposure to fluctuations in these costs. You might want to consider getting interest rate protection to lower your risk of volatile changes that could impact your long-term rates on accounts when they are at their lowest.

## *Tax Strategies*

A good relationship with your bank can also help you save up on your taxes. They can offer you practical advice on how best to execute real estate transactions to give you significant tax advantages.

For example, they may suggest a tax-deferred property exchange where you can swap one piece of property for another of similar value, all while deferring the need to pay federal income taxes until you are ready. In such a case, the income tax for the exchange of property would not be due until the stuff you received in the deal is sold, and you have a lot more money in your account to pay them.

## *Lines of Credit*

Another way you can work with your bank is through a line of credit. While you may get your funding from any number of sources, you will still have to pay for your expenses through your bank account. You can establish a regular line of credit through them to cover any costs related to property renovations, the closing costs, and other expenses that will be a part of your business. A small company with a strong credit history and a long-standing relationship with their bank can go a lot further than one that is bouncing from one account to another.

## *Mortgage Loans*

Unless you have loads of cash in hand, you're probably going to need to get a mortgage to pay for your properties. If you're doing traditional financing, you'll need to have a good relationship with your bank. Attempt to know as much as you can about how the bank handles mortgages before choosing a bank. Because real estate mortgages are likely the highest form of income for the bank, you want to know what kind of relationship they can offer. If you can forge a solid bond, it can be a win-win for both parties. Don't accept their first offer but be willing to negotiate for a better interest rate, more manageable payment plans, and lower fees. Don't accept if the terms are not right for you.

# Location, Location, Location

Location is always the key to any investment, whether it is your home or a rental. You have a choice to buy locally or try your hand at private assets. There are advantages and disadvantages to both approaches, which you need to understand before you move forward.

Buying local can provide you with a competitive advantage over other investors, particularly those who will be absentee landlords. The average person already has a wealth of knowledge about their community, which can help invest in the correct properties. You also have intimate knowledge of the market and proximity to the rental, which can help you overcome any disadvantage you might face in a less than an attractive marketplace. Of course, there are numerous reasons you might be compelled to invest in a private market, and you will need to take extraordinary efforts to mitigate the disadvantages of not being local.

## Why Location is Important?

If you watch any of the HGTV shows or go to a seminar about real estate, the first thing you ask is why location is imperative to buying property. The place has to do with value and property type. You already learned that certain property types are easier for you to invest in and better returns on your investment. As you assess the location, you also ask if the home is a worthwhile investment or if you are just throwing money at it.

Location is about the purchase price, value, and your intentions. Value is assessed based on the purpose of the property. The main home can increase in value over your life, whereas a rental property might need to gain value quicker so you can enjoy the equity. Value for an investor is based on income production and ROI.

Flippers or speculators wish for a quick profit, so they look at an undervalued property that will be bought and sold at a better value.

Location determines value, whether something is undervalued, and will remain that way for a long time or will gain it quickly with a few updates. The land is not something you can move, obviously, but you could pick up a house from its foundation and set it somewhere else, at significant expense—the point—location sets the value. Topographically speaking, higher-valued homes tend to be in the city center. Those who cannot afford the city center must commute at least 30 minutes, if not closer to an hour, just to have a place they can afford. As new, small shopping communities develop and more neighborhoods and schools increase, homes' values also increase, despite the long commute.

Denver and the Denver International Airport (DIA) area is an example of how communities can begin at a lower value and explode with development. When the airport moved from Stapleton to become larger and handle more air traffic, nothing was around it. After almost 30 years, DIA is now like a city of its own, with numerous neighborhoods. Housing costs went from around $100,000 up to $150,000 to more than $350,000. The new builds are closer to $400,000 and half a million. The older homes are being bought, flipped, and then sold at similar prices.

If they bought their homes, the families who could afford to live there could still survive and work around the airport and many new stores and hotels. However, those who rented are having to look at places in lower rent neighborhoods, closer to the old Colfax area, which tends to have gangs and crime. The apartment complexes are pushing out the low to middle- income families due to the competitive rental costs.

As possible, tenants move away from the city centers and new shopping centers that make mini villages, the prices continue to lower, but the commute cost has to account for the expenses one pays.

Assessing the location and value is imperative to choosing the right property for your intentions as the investor and must rely on economic changes.

### *Price to Rent Ratio*

Calculations and formulas are always going to use, and it applies as much to the location talk as our earlier discussion on money to be made from rental property investments.

The price to rent ratio equals average property price divided by average annual rent, equal to the average property price divided by the average monthly rent times 12.

Let's say the average property price in Los Angeles is

$812,571, and the average monthly rent is $3,324. The price to rent ratio for Los Angeles would be $812,571/ ($3,324 x 12). The result is 20 for the cost to rent ratio. But what does this mean for you? A low price to rent ratio is between zero and 15. Average ratios are 16 to 20, with high being anything over 21.

The rent is a comparison between whether it is a property to buy or rent. A lower ratio shows the prices are low compared to the average rent you can receive, versus a high price to rent rate, where the property sells for more than you can probably rent it. A moderate number can show it is an okay rental or too high and is better for a long-term purchase investment. An average market makes it hard to tell what should happen. However, most experts, including me, believe you would be able to rent the property more than someone would be willing to buy it.

You do not want to use this metric as the only deciding factor about location. You want to use it to determine the average rent and whether you could gain that much in the area you are considering buying.

You can find as much information as you need to complete the calculation based on the city you are researching. Mashvisor is one website, but many tell you where to get city-data regarding the U.S. housing market. You also have the opportunity to find investment property calculators, neighborhood pages, and information to help with the average property price and rental income amount

## *What are the Best Websites to Research Location?*

You want to use websites that will provide the data you need with trusted sources. The top three include neighborhooddiscount.com, realtor.com, and nar.realtor. However, if you want to know about population size and demographics, unemployment rate, household income, housing prices, interest rates, or daily traffic counts, refer to the data sources below.

• Population size and demographics - U.S. Census Bureau (census.gov)

- Unemployment rate - Bureau of Labor Statistics (bls.gov)

- Household income - Bureau of Labor Statistics (bls.gov) & U.S. Census Bureau (bls.gov)

- Housing prices - FRED economic research; HUD (fred.stlouisfed.org) (hud.gov)

- Interest rates - FRED economic research (fred.stlouisfed.org)

- Daily traffic counts - Data.gov

- Public schools - Data.gov

- Building permits - Data.gov & Local city offices

- Commercial real estate sales - Costar (costar.com) & LoopNet (loopnet.com)

The list above provides the type of data you require and notice you may have to view more than one website to find all the information you want. For example, daily traffic counts, public schools, and building permits can be found at data.gov, whereas demographics are accessible by the government's census website.

# Conclusion

Everything starts with your real estate story and goes from there. Once you know who you are, you need to start finding realtors, wholesalers, contractors, and money sources. You don't look for these one at a time; you look for all of them at once. This business only happens if you do it. You hold the keys to your success. It will always be easier for you to do the things that you have to do.

You have to go to work in the morning. You have to go grocery shopping. You have to rake the yard. If you don't do the things that I outlined here in this book, will your boss yell at you in the morning?

Will the dinner table be empty when you get home? Will the leaves pile up in your yard? Will I come to your home and yell at you?

No, none of these things will happen. You will continue your life as it is. It is always more challenging to do the items that don't have consequences. Things like contacting realtors to start sending you deals, picking a market to invest in, running numbers on properties, connecting with other investors; if you don't do these things, your life won't change. You will continue down the path you are on. However, if you put the time and energy into this business, if you decide to do the extra work instead of watching the game or taking a nap, your path will change. I believe that you can do this. I have seen people start with nothing and become real estate rock stars.

However, it takes many nights of hard work to become an overnight success.

When you get frustrated or hit a bump in the road, don't give up. Reach out to your network and ask for help—you don't have to do this alone

So, you can start achieving the results you want. Instead of a real estate– investing crash course that just provided a floor, walls, and ceilings, you now have your structure and doors and windows, cabinets and countertops, flooring, and lights.

This book contains many of the missing pieces most other educations don't provide or try to provide at break-the-bank pricing. Use what you have read. Use this flipping blueprint to build your future. You hold the power of the future in your hands. You decide which path you want to go down. Follow through with what was taught here, and you too can reclaim your time and achieve financial freedom.

# About the Author

Neal Hooper is an entrepreneur, investor and the author of bundle "Investing in Real Estate".

A leading authority figure in the world of business, money, finance, and wealth management. He graduated with honors in computer engineering and economics and lives with his wife Kristen in Los Angeles, CA.

Real estate has made him more money than he could ever have imagined, and now, he wants to give back to society. He has decided to put his experiences on paper and started writing books so that everyone gets an opportunity to benefit from his success.

Through his training and coaching programs, he has worked directly with thousands of aspiring investors to jumpstart their rental property journey.

Previously, Neal worked in several corporate real estate and finance roles at large private companies, including at a private equity investment firm covering a wide range of commercial real estate acquisitions.

He will guide you on your journey to financial freedom and early retirement.

CPSIA information can be obtained
at www.ICGtesting.com
Printed in the USA
BVHW062334010321
601388BV00009B/1056